April's Sister

by

Essie Sapp

ISBN: 0-75963-594-3

This book is printed on acid free paper.

1stBooks – rev. 05/22/01

In memory of my sister, Petrolla (Pat) Freeman.

 Dedicated to my sisters, Stell, Lucille, Rose, Jeanette and neice/sister, Pam.

I thank the following people for your support and encouragement:

Friend and soul-mate, David A. Benson, sons, Lamont and Artemus.

Fellow members of 'Urban Class Writers' Group, Michael Johnson, April Yenson, and Barbara Mackey. Thanks to Gwen Russell Green for putting us together.

My Sisters of the Sister Circle/Book Club:

Laurie Cohen, Jacqueline Harris, Vickie Harris, Sandra Powell, Teresa Sanders and Chandra L. White.

Thanks to:

Gwen Martin, Valerie (The Queen) Underwood for their humor and inspiration, also Lynda Hall and the other fine people at Fulton Co. Dept. of Family and Children Services.

Special thanks to Jacqueline Harris for her editorial assistance, patience and friendship, not necessarily in that order.

Essie Sapp

CECIL WITH A SHORT E

Essie Sapp

My marriage to Alphonso Youngblood hadn't been made in heaven and I guess you could say my divorce came from a place a good deal warmer. Still, I knew in my heart that it hadn't been all his fault. Thanks to my support group I began to understand that the scars from my marriage were just the surface eruption of wounds which went much deeper into the past. Still, my best friend, Sherry McElroy, was constantly trying to get me to date. But at forty-one, I thought, what the hell would I do on a date? I'd been away from that scene much too long. Instead, I chose to try and reconnect with my spirituality, I began attending church again. Joining the support group was a natural progression. Gradually the rituals and conformity that had turned me away from organized religion began to have new meaning. I felt like a baby taking tiny steps, a little fearful, yet determined.

One morning I was awakened by a voice in dialogue. It spoke to me in eloquent tones, using words of high intelligence not normal to everyday

3

speech. I had the sense that this voice had been speaking to me in a dream and had defied reality by continuing after I awoke. I remember feeling surprised that I wasn't amazed at all of this at the time. But I heard this; "Embrace your uniqueness, it's important. Accept your rightful place, your tiny part which fits perfectly in the puzzle and begin the thing you were put here to do. Acknowledge your scars, accept them."

I shifted my weight in bed, my eyes rested on a little cobweb clinging to the corner of the ceiling. It made sense. As if someone was giving me permission to be myself, as if someone was saying, "You're not perfect, but you do matter, so get on with it." I jumped out of bed and opened the blinds and my bedroom basked in the golden sunlight. I lifted my hands prayerfully, "Thanks," I said softly.

With this heightened state of consciousness, I knew that I had work to do before I could function in a satisfying relationship.

But Sherry was relentless. "What Quentin and I have is rare. Everyone says we have a 'good marriage'. I know I haven't done a damn thing to deserve it, but it's true, we do. I guess I'd just like to see you with someone who makes you happy, girl."

I knew she meant it, that's why I loved her.

One Saturday, after we'd jogged through her subdivision, sweat drying beneath our sportswear, Sherry started in on me again.

"He works for Atlanta Life with Quentin, Jo."

We were lounging in her spacious kitchen. Sherry sat slouched at the table, her pretty face resting in her hands. I once told her that she was an older version of Whitney Houston except she was fifteen or twenty pounds heavier.

"You remind me of Oprah with that fusion of luscious hair and the way you're always trying to renew yourself," she had responded. "But girl, I wish I had Whitney's money."

I'd given her one of my looks and we'd both laughed contemplating Oprah's money.

"Anyway, his name is Cecil Jamison. He's a lawyer. And," she held up her hand before I could speak, "it was Quentin's idea."

This was a new approach and I knew immediately that it was bull. If anything Sherry had bullied him into it. I poured fresh coffee at the counter.

"It won't kill me," I said.

"Then you'll meet him?"

"The group thinks I should get out some." I ran my hand over the cool Formica, examining its texture, trying to 'live in the moment' as the group advocated. It was firm and smooth like the back of a well-built man. Thinking these thoughts made me feel foolish and I turned and leaned against it with my coffee.

"And they're right. Nothing wrong with having a good time while you get yourself together."

"One woman, Lena, said we should all try and live more consciously, appreciate the little things. You know what I'm saying?"

Sherry yawned, ignoring me. "I'm thinking…the Frat club…Friday, we'll let Quentin handle it."

* * *

Quentin and Sherry were already in their favorite seats near the band when I arrived that Friday night. Cecil, looking quite dapper, arrived shortly after.

"Johanna, very nice, very nice indeed." His dark velvet eyes took me in slowly and he bowed slightly as Quentin introduced us.

"Cecil Jamison, Cecil with a short E," he said. His teeth were extravagantly white when he smiled and I couldn't help but notice how well his peanut-butter complexion blended with his ivory-colored suit.

Cecil wasted no time. He gazed directly into my eyes when he spoke as though we were two people

7

alone and throughout the evening he'd lean close to whisper in my ear and small talk soon gave way to intimacy. I found myself having a good time. A casual observer would easily have mistaken us for lovers. It was one of those rare occasions when everything seemed to come together naturally. The soft jazz, the wine. Just enough of this, just enough of that, like a perfectly blended cheesecake. When Sherry and I rose to go to the ladies' room, Cecil stood and held my chair like a gentleman. I was impressed.

* * *

"Cecil with a short E." Sherry grinned at me in the mirror as I applied fresh lipstick. "Girl, I'll bet you that this Nubian is from Tupelo, Mississippi or somewhere else just as country and his momma used to come out on the porch yelling, 'Ceeecil, Ceeecil! Get your little barefooted ass in this house boy!' Probably ran around in the dirt with no shoes until he started school. Talking about 'Cecil with a short E'. Please." We both cracked up laughing.

"If the brother really had it going on, the fucking E wouldn't matter, now would it?"

"You've got to admit though, girl, the brother does have style." I snapped my purse shut.

"You like him, huh?"

"He's alright." I averted my eyes, wary of Sherry's scrutiny. "Maybe a little too perfect...but nice." I wasn't ready to trust my feelings yet, let alone share them with Sherry.

"You seem to be enjoying yourself and the man is doing very well for himself.... divorced, no kids and fine to boot, girl." Sherry batted her eyes smugly and patted her shoulder-length hair in the mirror.

"Yeah, but you know me, flash and cash don't get it for me. Can't base a relationship on that. In the group we…"

"You're driving me crazy with that group-shit. You're forty-one years old, girl." Sherry lowered her voice as we exited the bathroom. "You'd better get with the program."

I fell in step with her as we maneuvered through the crowded club.

"This group means a lot to me, Sher, it's really helped me."

"Why don't you just go to church?"

"I need it all, I embrace it all. I'm learning to face my fears, you know?"

"What fears, girl?"

"Everything."

"Oh God, this is about the rape. I know where this is going."

"Not the rape, my rape, okay?" Sometimes Sherry seemed so callous to me.

"Okay, so it was your rape. And excuse me if I'm politically incorrect, but I don't see any point in you rehashing your past all the damn time. I mean, haven't most women been raped one way or the other? Mind-fucked? Men too for that matter. Some women are raped by their own husbands. You've got to let it go, Jo."

"You just don't understand," I said.

Cecil sprang to his feet as we approached the table. As if on cue, the band swung into a soft slow tune. Cecil nodded toward the dance floor and held out his hand. I went willingly and drifted dreamily with the music in his cozy embrace. My forehead tingled where his trim goatee lightly stroked it. I closed my eyes and inhaled his spicy scent and the hint of gin at his throat.

At the table across from us, Quentin winked at Sherry as he fiddled with his cigar. He looked pleased with himself in his new role as matchmaker. Sherry smiled and touched his face lightly. He caught her hand and held it. They were in their own world.

Serenity surrounded me, I raised my head with a smile for Cecil, aware that he was watching me. The intensity in his eyes was startling. My blissful state dissipated into tiny bubbles like flat champagne. I turned away.

"Don't," he said, lifting my face. "Look at me." His deep brown eyes had softened. He raised my hand to his mouth and kissed the tips of my fingers.

"You intrigue me. I'd like to see you again." He pressed his face in the hollow of my neck and breathed deeply the way you sniff freshly washed clothes.

"I'd like that," I said. I realized that I meant it. I dismissed the anguish or whatever it was I'd seen in his eyes a moment ago. I told myself I was being overly sensitive because I hadn't been this close to a man in such a long time.

The music quickened into a reggae beat. Cecil grinned and before I knew it began twirling me around the floor faster and faster as if he was John Travolta in "Saturday Night Fever". Eyes fastened on us and people stood aside anticipating a show. I went for it. I wasn't a dancer but Cecil was a natural, so in honor of my new consciousness, I danced like no one was watching, my inhibitions gone. I felt wonderful. Cecil dipped and twisted me around until we were both exhilarated. The crowd clapped and demanded, "Go head, go head." Finally, laughing and exhausted, I managed to drag Cecil off the dance floor.

At the end of the evening, he asked when we'd get together again. From pure habit I hesitated.

"With your friends again...if you want." He observed me closely. "I don't want to give you an excuse to say no."

* * *

Later that night, I awoke drenched in perspiration. My heart pounded in rhythm with the refrigerator motor which seemed unnaturally loud. In my dream I'd been surrounded by huge rats, I couldn't recall the entire thing, but a fearful part lingered at my mind's edge and in my mind's eye, a rat squeezed itself under my bedroom door, it's muscles and bones collapsing and expanding like a cartoon. I shivered and shook my head clear. Calmed a bit, I got up, flipped on the lights and dashed back into bed like a child. I lay there for a time listening for dreaded skittish movement of tiny feet before finally drifting off.

The next morning I slept late, warm thoughts of the night before filled me, the dream long gone.

* * *

The following week Sherry and I decided on the blues show at the Omni after debating whether she and Quentin should go.

"Do you really need a chaperone with this guy?"

I'd given it some thought. "No, but I'd like to keep things light. Besides, he suggested that you two come."

"Come on, Jo, you know he'd rather be alone with you."

"Let's just leave it like it is." I didn't want to make a big deal out of it one way or the other.

* * *

Quentin picked up tickets for everyone and on Saturday night Cecil and I met the McElroys at the theater.

"Over here," Sherry shouted, her hand waved above the crowd. We were in the lobby. Quentin led us to our seats near the front. The show was starting.

The air was thick with Marijuana and the potent smell of beer. The open bar was a joke. People brought their own libations. I adjusted my eyes to the darkness, silver and green shakers glowed and twinkled in unseen hands. I was reminded of the psychedelic seventies.

Sherry and I got into the groove, screaming and shouting like fools as the group took us back in time. We were seated between the two men.

15

Quentin was his usual laid-back self, above the fray, but relaxed and smiling as his shoulders moved with the music. Cecil leaned away slightly, stiff and silent with no apparent interest in the show. But I didn't think much of it at the time.

I nudged Sherry in the side, "Remember when we used to sneak into the Elks?"

Sherry grinned, "Yeah girl, we were some fast little things."

I pictured the two of us back home in Genesis, Ohio, a notorious little city outside of Cleveland, when we were teenagers. Sherry and I went way back and though we approached life from different angles, somehow we were on the same plane. There wasn't much we hadn't shared over the years. She was a self-proclaimed realist who accepted life as it came. 'Go with the flow' had always been her motto. I, on the other hand, examined myself constantly. Sherry said I was 'deep'. Yet as friends, we were like ice cream and cake. She and Quentin were the reason I'd moved to

Atlanta after my divorce. They'd relocated five years earlier.

"Atlanta is the Black Mecca," she'd said.

"We were something else, weren't we?" I said. We laughed and high-fived each other as though we were still teenagers. Quentin grinned at us and shook his head.

Cecil seized my elbow suddenly. "You're here with me remember? I hate to see you women get all worked up over these entertainment people." He threw his head back, took a swig from his silver flask, grimaced and wiped his mouth with the back of his hand.

"Hey loosen up, we're just trying to have a little fun." I was surprised at his attitude. He retreated to the far side of his seat, sulking.

"He's a little uptight, isn't he?" Sherry whispered.

"Maybe this just isn't his thing," I said. I didn't want to get Sherry started, she could kill a dead horse.

"Oh yeah, I forgot, he is Cecil with a short E. Mr. 'Crème de la Crème'. But if you ask me, he's had too much of that damn gin. What kind of brother drinks gin, anyway? Gin is for 'ooold ass' fools."

"Cool it Sherry, maybe the guy just don't like the blues," said Quentin. He sat forward and peered at Cecil. "Hey man, maybe we could ride out to your place and check out some of that great jazz after the show. Didn't you tell me you have a dynamite 'Miles' collection?"

"Yeah, yeah, yeah." Cecil didn't even bother to look at Quentin.

We tried to enjoy the remainder of the show, but the mood had changed. I became self-conscious, aware of Cecil's sullen stare.

Before long, the band began a medley of songs, an indication that the show would soon end and people started leaving to avoid the throng that would soon ensue.

"I'd better go to the ladies' room before we leave," said Sherry.

I stood, intending to follow her, but Cecil grabbed my arm again. This irritated me.

"Let's get some air," he said.

Before I could protest, he ushered me toward the aisle as he slipped his flask into his back pocket and smoothed his jacket over it. I stepped over Quentin's feet to reach the aisle. Behind me, Cecil bent and whispered in his ear. Quentin's brows formed two steeples.

"Okay man, w'll catch up with you guys. You okay babe?" He searched my face. I nodded as someone bumped against me. "Excuse me, excuse me," they said. I glanced backwards as Cecil whisked me through the crowd.

"Let's wait for them."

"They're coming," Cecil said.

Outside the theater I took a deep breath. Atlanta was warmer than usual for this time of year. People were in light jackets, but not me. The crisp air felt good on my arms. The night was bright with Christmas lights. In front of the theater stood a small replica of the splendid tree on Peachtree Street downtown. The smell of pine and popcorn and delicious foods from nearby restaurants wafted through the air. It was my favorite time of year, but right then, I was agitated.

Cecil, what's the hurry?" His face was hidden as he walked briskly.

"I've got something I want you to see."

I hung behind him, feeling slightly off balance. When we reached his white Volvo, a brother lounged casually against the front fender smoking, a sign hung around his chiseled neck which read 'Will work for food'.

"Move it man," Cecil said, not breaking his stride as he went to the driver's side. "I ain't got time for your shit."

In the moonlight of the lot, the man's dread locks were blue-black and I could see that he was quite handsome despite his dirty clothes and the odor of despair about him. I opened my clutch bag fumbling for a dollar for the homeless brother. The motor of the Volvo started quietly, and Cecil motioned for me to get in. his chivalry act had all but disappeared. As I stepped gingerly through the gravel around the car, the homeless brother began moving rhythmically, his dreads flopping, he broke into a rap:

God made the sun
God made the rain
But when he made you
Beautiful black lady
He made a beautiful thang

I smiled and shoved two dollar bills into the brother's hands. For an instant, I wondered what his story was. Everybody had one.

I climbed into the Volvo, obviously Cecil wanted a little time alone with me. He hadn't enjoyed the show, but we'd had such fun together that first night, I was certain he had an explanation. He'd tell me that he'd had a really bad day…or something. The moment I closed the car door, he gunned the motor and screeched out of the parking lot like a hyped teenager.

"Cecil, I thought we…"

"Relax, babe, we're just going to my place."

In the rear-view mirror, the street brother was etched in the shadows, his hands outstretched as if beckoning me back.

"I hipped Quentin," Cecil continued, "they're coming. Just relax, s'gonna be nice. Listen to some mellow jazz, know what I mean? Then maybe you can get excited about me, n'stead of some clown up on the fuckin' stage." His mouth twitched involuntarily and his speech was slurred. He was wasted. He sipped from his flask, narrowed his eyes and attempted to concentrate on the road.

"Put this in the glove compartment." He shoved the flask at me, eyes still on the road. I obeyed and lowered my window. The gin smell was like strong medicine. From the corner of my eye, I glared at him. This was the part I hated…when a brother changed up on you. I'd been too stupid, too hopeful, in spite of all my consciousness-raising, to see it coming.

* * *

We were outside the city limits. A Gwinnett county sign loomed past. This area was unfamiliar to me. I cursed myself for not watching the road, it was a habit of mine not to watch where I was going unless I was doing the driving. A bad habit. The possibility that I could be in danger welled up in me and my stomach, my weakest part, began to knot. All I could see was the vague outline of huge pines racing by. I lit a Benson & Hedge to calm down. The ash tray squeaked when I pulled it out. Cecil's head jerked, he seemed startled. Abruptly, he turned off onto an unpaved road and made a sharp right up a steep, unlit driveway. I turned, desperately seeking my friends' car behind us.

Cecil jumped from the car without saying anything when we reached the house. He didn't bother to open the door for me. I had no choice, I got out of the car and followed him. For the second time that night, I cursed myself: I'd left my cellular phone at home on the bureau.

A musty smell hit me when Cecil opened the door. The house was misty black inside.

"Let there be light," I said, hoping I sounded regular, confident. The heavy door slammed and everything became silent, as if we'd just shut out the entire world. My breathing became heavy. I fumbled for a light switch. Click. Nothing. Panicking, I stretched forth my hand, "Cecil!"

"Shut up bitch!"

He snatched my arm and restrained me, as his free hand opened the blinds. Moonlight shown on an antique-looking sofa.

"Get this shit off."

He grabbed a handful of my silk dress and ripped it. Stunned, I stood there with my dress hanging from me.

"Please, please Cecil, you're drunk. Don't do this."

"Come on."

He tried to drag me but I refused to move. With one quick yank, my feet were uprooted and he dragged me across the room. The air changed and I knew we were in the bedroom. He loosened his grip momentarily and lifted something from a dresser, then turned back on me and silently, swiftly, he slit my disheveled clothes right down the middle, underwear and all, with what must've been a straight razor. Then he stood back a moment to admire his handiwork I suppose. I couldn't see his eyes but I sensed that same hunger I'd glimpsed the night we met, when I'd danced so freely in his arms. But now he was like a shadowy figure who'd changed from Dr. Jekyll to Mr. Hyde – straight out of one of my childhood nightmares. More frightening than that first time…

No one heard my screams when he invaded me. Angry, he withdrew and hit me in the face with his fist. An intense whiteness flashed before me and I felt the heat of my face swelling before I passed out.

* * *

Light spilled into the room and I hurt all over. Wearily, my eyes followed the light. The source was a tiny blue lamp, like a child's, on the nightstand. I knew Cecil was in the room. In a moment his clammy hands caressed my swollen cheek. I winced and with great effort, turned to face him. His eyes shined down on me as if I was his beloved bride or something. My stomach heaved and I swallowed hard to keep from throwing up. My body felt as if it was lifeless.

"You're afraid of me now, aren't you?"

His voice was melancholy as he searched my face. Something – instinct made me whisper, "No, I'm not afraid."

"Yes, yes you are." He nodded as if he had the final say.

By this time I realized my friends weren't coming and I couldn't believe how naïve I'd been. I tried to read his face, *Would he let me go?*

Once, I'd seen a movie where this woman was raped and afterwards, in fear of her life and sensing she was dealing with a psychopath, she'd cleverly hidden her fear and pretended she'd enjoyed it. Strangely, this had deflated the man, but he didn't harm her further. Instead, he'd leapt away like a wounded animal, as if somehow, 'he'd' been offended.

Nauseated, I reached out and caressed Cecil's temple. I was desperate. He jumped like he'd been shocked. He turned abruptly on his side, his back to me, with his head propped against his hand. Warily, I watched the muscles stretch in his back as he opened a drawer. There was a click. He turned in full view, slung the gun around in his hand, his eyes narrowed at me. He nodded as if he'd reached a decision. I lay there in terror, unable to move. From out of nowhere, I heard my Mom's voice: *"Don't be too trusting, Jo. This can be an evil world, honey."* The bed moaned as he lay down heavily on his back, clutching the gun to his chest, the barrel staring at me. In the silence I heard a low hissing sound, like a tea kettle boiling. God! He was laughing – laughing through clenched teeth. In the moonlight his pupils were brilliant, like the eyes of a black cat I once cornered in my grandmother's basement.

As I lay there frozen in fear, the dream I'd had the night I met cecil came to me in full force.

I was running, running toward a dark cave. Echos, voices calling my name. Behind me, chasing me were huge gray rats, so many I couldn't count, closing in on me. A male voice called out to me. I knew the voice, feared it mightily. It came closer and closer. One of the rats ran along side of me, gnawing on something he'd killed. I stopped in my tracks, horrified. His little face was covered with blood. A pungent odor filled the air. The rats were at my heels. The dreaded voice was at my ear. I turned to face him, trapped, terrified. At that moment, I woke up.

Now I knew that the dream had been a warning about Cecil. The voice was Cecil's.

Cecil's snoring brought me back to the present. Incredibly, he'd fallen asleep, gun still in hand. I knew that if I was going to escape, I had to make my move. Slowly, forgetting my pain, I lifted myself. All the while, I was watching Cecil. Stealthily, I eased out of the bed. Cecil shifted and I froze. I stole a look at him, his mouth twitched but he was still asleep. I moved cautiously to the head of the bed to look at him. He no longer gripped the gun tight, it was just laying there on his chest, his hand resting near it.

I didn't hesitate. I snatched up the gun and gripped it tightly, ready for anything. Cecil grunted and turned on his side facing me, his breathing slow. He was still asleep. The gun felt heavy and alien in my hands. I clutched it tighter as I backed away from the bed. My thoughts raced as I stood transfixed. I imagined myself shooting – legs spread wide as I backed out the door. Blood everywhere, the fear in his eyes, I'd need to see that. Then I'd shoot the kid who raped me when I was sixteen…my hands were shaking.

"What'd that boy do to you, baby?" Mom's arms *had reached for me, her voice soothing.*

I told her Billie Echols did it. We all went downtown, me and Mom and Billie and his mom. Neither of our fathers came.

"They're both just kids," the juvenile lady had said. "We don't want to ruin these kid's lives, best to let it go." Mom had agreed. I think they gave Billie probation or something. It was all very quiet and I

*was in a daze. I never spoke about it again to anyone
but Sherry.*

Oh yes, I could kill you, I thought. I was overcome
with rage and had to cover my mouth to keep from
screaming as I pictured Cecil smiling insanely, white
even teeth gleaming in the dark. Finally though, I
came to my senses.

"Fuck you Cecil. Fuck you and all your kind.
You're not worth it."

I snatched up my torn dress and wrapped it around
me as best I could, and grabbed my heels, there was no
use putting them on. With gun in hand, I crept toward
the bedroom door in a crouch, still watching the bed,
praying as I turned the knob. God was with me, the
old door didn't creak or whine. I didn't bother to close
it. Like a cat in the night, I leapt silently through the
living room and opened the door. The cool night air
aggravated the tender side of my face as I raced down
the driveway. Gravel pushed sharply against the
bottom of my feet. A door slammed somewhere, but I

moved faster, never looking back. I don't remember when or where the gun slipped from my hand.

* * *

Above the tall pines, daylight moved in slowly as I stumbled through the woods. Crickets quieted down so the birds could do their morning thing. The sound of an occasional motor told me I was nearing a highway. I stopped to catch my breath, thankful for the daylight. I leaned against an old tree to examine my feet. They were bruised and wounded from the rocks and gravel but miraculously no glass had wedged into any of the wounds. All the cool air in the world couldn't erase the smell of Cecil though. I smelled him all around me. I bent and threw up hard, supporting myself against the tree as I took in great gulps of air. Then I moved on.

When the trees cleared and the highway loomed brightly, I kept close to the woods whenever a car drove by. I was half-naked and unable to trust another man on this day. I stumbled on for what seemed an eternity, cold and weary. I felt no pain though, my body was numb. I just kept moving and as I walked, my head slowly cleared and I only knew one thing – he wouldn't get away with it, not this time. I could take some comfort in that.

* * *

Still deep in though, I hadn't seen the Gwinnett County cruiser pull along the curb. But then someone shouted, "Jo, Johanna, are you all right?" It was Sherry. They had pulled behind the cruiser.

"Oh my God, look at her Quentin. I told you something wasn't right. I told you!"

"Stop it Sherry, not now." Quentin was already out of the car. He took off his jacket as he rushed toward me and threw it around my shoulders. He avoided my eyes, as we approached the cruiser, I knew he felt bad, that he would try to shoulder the blame. But I wasn't going to let him, no matter what Sherry said. He was good people. Always had been.

THE TRAP

April's Sister

"You're dead, man," Warren said. Frightened by his own voice, his eyes darted around in his head. To his left he saw an I-85 sign. At least he knew where he was, to his right was Rawson St. It was in the wee hours of the morning and he was lying on his back on the slant under the bridge on Pryor St. A broken grocery cart lay on its side, its wheels facing him like an expectant lover. The fancy lampposts that had been erected for the '96 Olympics were all busted out. A moonbeam peered down at him, where the bridge parted, casting an eerie shadow. All was quiet except for the light rain pelting the scattered leaves on the sidewalk below. Warren nearly jumped out of his skin when a beer can rolled off the slant down into the street; clank-clank, clank, clank.

Warren closed his weary eyes. A red ant crept up his leg and he slapped and scratched. A cigarette butt fell from his nappy hair as he cushioned his hands under his head and straightened his legs. He hadn't changes clothes for days and his scent mingled with the smell of the worms that oozed from the moistened earth beneath the cracked cement.

"Tracy loves you, man. How's she gonna feel when they find you in a place like this – stinking, crawling with bugs and shit – or worse – shot down like a dog over a lousy piece of crack cocaine."

"Stop it," Warren said.

"And Sharon, your baby, working on her Masters, trying to make you proud…"

"Shut the fuck up," Warren said. He sat up with difficulty, his lower back on fire with pain. He thought of 'Little Man' over in the trap; walking up and down MLK, riding the train, gesturing, talking to himself like a madman. The contempt he used to have for him. He thought of himself, how he was no longer himself. He sucked in damp air, lowered his head and cried.

The rain slowed to a drizzle and Warren finally gripped the side of the grocery cart and raised himself up from the wet pavement. He had to walk back through the trap to get home, it was the shortcut but he wasn't even sure if he could make it. He'd been out there five days chasing the rock. When his money had run out on the third day, he'd started hustling, doing whatever he could to get another hit. As usual, Shorty had let him handle a little business. He'd smoked up some of that too, but he knew Shorty wouldn't hurt him. Shorty would let him slide. Shorty was the only dealer in the trap that knew Warren had a background in finance and knew his shit. This gave Shorty an edge. Warren had tightened him up many times, shown him a thing or two. So he could look over some things – as long as Warren didn't try to punk him out. Warren didn't, he had to survive out there. Shorty was his man.

He crept along Ralph David Abernathy, blending with the shadows, cold and hungry, he didn't remember the last time he'd eaten. But he moved swiftly, aware that he was an easy target for whatever went down. Earlier in the day, he hadn't cared, had almost wished someone would waste his sorry ass. He was so tired of being tired of his own shit. But then there was Tracy – and his daughter. And there was something in him too, that wanted desperately to escape this twilight zone. He'd tried many times. But each time he'd establish some clean time and was able to look at just how far down the ladder he'd climbed, everyday problems would seem overwhelming, and he'd just say "fuck it". He'd straddle the fence for awhile until he was right back into the maze, groping to find his way back again. He had a recurring dream of being trapped in a deep well, anguished voices echoing all around him, darkness surrounding him. He wished to God he could find some peace.

At the corner of MLK and Ralph David Abernathy, he found a well-lit phone booth. Two women eyed him from the parking lot across the street as he fumbled for change. He recognized the light-skinned sister as Frieda the Freak – strung out bad. She'd be in

41

his face if he didn't keep moving. At that moment, a grizzly looking guy approached the women and Warren ducked into the booth. He only found a dime in his pocket, an operator had to put him through.

"Tracy, it's Warren, baby. I just wanted you to know that I'm alright." He heard a deep sigh.

"I've been going nuts, Warren. Where are you? You promised you were going back to treatment. Where are you?"

Warren stalled, afraid his voice would crack. "I... Tracy, let's not do this over the phone. I just wanted you to know that I'm okay and I'm coming home." He held his breath.

"No, you can't come home, don't even try. You probably need to be monitored. Go to Grady. I can't take care of you when you're like this and you know it."

"I know how you feel Trace, you know I do. But just for tonight. I'm cold and filthy. Let me come home and clean up, get some rest, that's all I'm asking." He couldn't tell her how hungry he was, he was too ashamed.

"You know how this scares me Warren…"

"Look, I'm okay, I'm stable. I just need some rest. I'll check back into treatment tomorrow morning; if I go to Grady hospital like this, they're not going to process me in for hours. They'll sit me on a hard bench until they change shifts, give me some stale crackers, you know how they operate, Trace."

"Alright Warren," Tracy said finally. "But if you don't go tomorrow…"

Warren hung up. He didn't really know how stable he was. He just knew that if his heart started acting up, he wanted to be near Tracy and if he had to be hospitalized, he wanted his body to be clean. He couldn't go out like that.

"Hey Warren, what's up, man? I need to holler at you, man," Frieda the Freak yelled.

"Trying to get somewhere, babe." Warren threw up his hands to ward her off as he exited the booth. "I'll catch up with you," he lied.

A Day and Night taxi raced past him as he stepped into the street, splashing muddy water in mid-air and all over his already sodden shoes.

* * *

It was pouring by the time Warren reached the apartment. Tracy made him put his smelly shoes on the patio. She'd made vegetable soup and turkey sandwiches for him. She went back to bed as soon as she was reasonably sure Warren wasn't in a crisis. She never tried to talk to him when he came in off of a binge like this. Warren knew she'd lie there listening and alert until he fell asleep or at least settled down. Later she'd tip down the stairs and check on him.

Warren forced himself to shower before he ate. In the shower he threw his head back, arched his body at every angle and let the hot water baptize him for as long as he could stand it. He got out, grateful that Tracy was in bed, he needed to eat alone. He took his hand and dipped the beef chunks out of the soup, and with his other, shoved one of the sandwiches into his mouth. He got another bowl of soup and some crackers from the cupboard, crumbled them into the soup, helped himself to another sandwich and then washed it all down with a half carton of milk. He thought of all the addicts over in the trap that by now had been kicked out of their respective crack houses because they'd run out of money and were now broke and hungry with no place to go. Only another addict could appreciate the meal and hot shower the way he did. He wished he could do something – maybe when he got straight…

* * *

He was already dressed when Tracy got up. He'd slept fitfully on the couch, cursing someone in his dream who'd short-changed him. Tracy had lain awake listening to him, she hadn't slept at all.

Dr. Melendez met them in the Mental Health Unit of the treatment center. She got right to the point. "It is not working at home. You are putting yourself at much risk." Her accent only added to her authoritative manner, but there was warmth also.

"You cannot continue taking all the meds you're taking for your heart, high blood and particularly the depression medication and binge on street drugs as well. You will kill yourself. You will have to work the program in-house. We will take it one day at a time. More than likely, we will place you in a half-way house upon release."

Tracy nodded in agreement. Warren said nothing; he was tired of resisting both of them. Always he'd hated the program – my name is Warren and I'm an addict – all that crap. And listening to all the war stories. But he had to admit, the program had given him some new insight and he'd met some really righteous brothers – and sisters as well, black and white. He would go back. He'd use other tools though, not just the program, there were many options. Anything was better than the twilight zone. Hell, he had no way to go but up. Yeah, my name is Warren and I AM an addict.

APRIL'S SISTER

Joey had been dead for about a week when April first saw her again. Like a colorful video, Joey appeared drifting toward her in slow motion. Joey's feet swam back and forth like the ebb and flow of the tide, beckoning April with something in her hand. As April peered closer, she saw that Joey's hand held a tiny bouquet of red roses. April was tempted to reach out and accept them, but something held her back – the fading in and out, the weaving and bobbing disconcerted and frightened her. She turned and ran the rest of the way home from school without looking back.

The night Joey got killed, April was awakened by the phone. In those days they only had one phone and that night it only rang once. Instinctively, April knew that Losie had answered it. She turned over and peered in her sister's bunk bed below and sure enough, it was empty. She knew Losie was downstairs in the closet off the living room where she'd probably been on the phone for hours. The phone cord would be stretched to its limit across the living-room floor, as she talked to her boyfriend. Billie said Losie was boy-crazy.

April heard Billie's bed creak and knew there would be hell to pay.

"Who was that Losie? You'd better not be down there on that phone this time of night with your little fast ass. What time is it anyway?" By this time Billie was half- way down the stairs.

"Did you hear me girl?" Billie asked.

April couldn't hear a response. She looked at the little radio clock on the nightstand. It was 12:35 a.m. Something wasn't right. April got up and went down the stairs. At the bottom of the stairwell, she wrapped herself around the railing and hung on to the banister. Even though she felt uneasy, she didn't want to get in Billie's way. Billie could be evil this time of night.

"Who was that on the phone," asked Billie.

Losie stood with the phone dangling awkwardly in her hand, eyes wide like someone who'd just seen a ghost.

"Answer me girl, what's wrong with you?"

"It's Joey, something's happened to Joey!" Losie's voice broke into tears.

"What happened?" asked April.

"What happened?' asked Billie. "Stop being a tomboy April, get off that banister. What are you saying, Losie?"

Losie sobbed quietly.

"What is it baby?" Billie made her voice gentle as she shook Losie.

April came off the stairway over to where Losie stood sobbing.

"Miss Mae said Boleo shot Joey. He shot Joey."

"What? No!" Billie looked confused. "Was that Mae on the phone, was that Mae?"

"Yes ma'am," Losie whispered.

"What happened?" April wailed. Her stomach did a flip-flop when Losie said the word 'shot'.

"She said… She said, 'who is this?' I said, 'This is Losie'. She said, 'Tell your mother Boleo just shot Jo Jo', kinda fast-like and she hung up."

Billie's legs began to tremble and April saw this and ran and dropped in front of her mother and clung to her legs so that they would stop shaking.

"Stop that, April," Billie snapped. "If you're not being a tom-boy, you're being a big baby. Both of you, help me find my keys. There's just been an accident, that's all. I've gotta get over there."

* * *

Ms. Barnett, April's best friend Renee's mother, and their closest neighbor, wouldn't let Billie drive.

"You ain't in no shape to be behind the wheel of a car." She made Billie sit while she called Jack, Billie's brother. Ms. Barnett stayed with the girls and made them eat pancakes.

When they went to their room, Losie flopped on her bunk and started to cry and April went to her and they huddled together in fear of the unknown. Soon Losie started snoring and April climbed into the top bunk and lay there staring at the ceiling. April smelled coffee and listened to the sounds of dishes clashing as Ms. Barnett moved around downstairs before she too dozed.

When April awoke, Losie was already downstairs somewhere. The house was filled with people. April's uncle Jack sat in the pantry across from Billie.

"Drink it," he said. "It ain't gonna hurt you. You've got to settle your nerves."

"This is your answer for everything, ain't it Jack," said Billie.

Jack lit his cigar. "Drink it Billie. This ain't no time for all that."

Billie picked up the shot glass and gulped the liquor down, grimacing as tears gushed from her eyes.

"Jack, that bastard killed my baby! He killed my little Jo Jo, Jack." Billie's head lolled into her hands.

April moved in to comfort her, but her Uncle snatched her up into his lap and cradled her in his chest. In the security of his arms, the smell of liquor, cigars and ivory soap, April was able to let go. She was her uncle's favorite and she knew that even though she was eleven years old, her uncle Jack wouldn't tell her to be a big girl, and he wouldn't care if she cried, so she did. He stroked her back gently as he stroked Billie with his words.

"We'll get through this Billie. You ain't even got to worry. They better not ever turn him loose cause I swear fo' God, I'll kill him." He patted Billie's shoulder, his eyes glassy. He shook his head as if to clear it. "I swear fo' God, I'll kill him."

April had never seen Billie cry before and it frightened her. Losie had told April that she had come home from school last year when President Kennedy was killed and found Billie crying, but April didn't believe it. Billie hadn't even cried when their daddy had died. Losie said she probably cried when they couldn't see her but April didn't believe that either. Her uncle always said, 'Your momma's as mean as a snake. Strong. Trust her with my life'. Then he'd tell stories about how Billie had killed snakes in the fields when they were growing up in the South and how she had stood up to their daddy (who was also mean as a snake) and even went and hauled their daddy out of juke joints single-handedly when he went on one of his frequent binges. That, April believed. She kept looking for cracks in Billie's armor. She found none. As long as Billie held up, she felt safe.

* * *

At the wake, Billie was glorious in her black suit and hat. She held her head high as her brother, Jack led her to the casket. If it hadn't been for the black sunglasses she wore to conceal her swollen eyes, she could have been attending an elegant affair. Billie didn't believe in showing out. Jack had told April and Losie that Billie would rather die herself before she let all those crazy-ass folks see her break down and act like a damn fool, just give them something else to talk about. "Your momma does her crying alone," he said.

At the casket, her brother stood back to allow Billie a moment. She stood there elegantly looking down on Joey, then she bent and kissed her lightly. It was all so quiet, April could hardly breathe watching her. Then Billie turned and held out her hand for Jack to lead her away.

April and Losie wouldn't let their Aunt Lucille lead them up the aisle, their Uncle Jack had to come and get them. He grasped their waist and pulled them firmly to his side at the casket. A sound erupted from deep inside him that terrified April. Then she looked inside the casket. Joey was swollen grotesquely and her face was a gaudy mask, like a sorrowful clown.

April broke away and ran blindly down the aisle of the church. Hands grasped for her, but she kept running until she felt the cool of the September air on her face.

After that, Billie wouldn't let them attend the funeral.

"Did you really want to go?" Losie asked April afterwards.

"No," April snapped. "That wasn't even Joey we saw anyway. She never looked like that. Why'd they make her look so weird like that? And she wasn't even hardly any bigger than us, right?"

"Yep." Losie's eyes welled up and she shook her head. "I heard Uncle Jack say something about the gun shot wounds making her swell. He said they did the best they could.

Uncle Jack says if they let Boleo out, he's going to kill him. You believe he'll kill him?"

"I hope so," said April, and she meant it.

Billie made them go to school that Monday even though Joey was buried on Saturday and they could have easily been excused.

"No need in you girls mopin' around here all day. You're both startin' new schools and you don't need to miss out on anything." April was starting junior high and Losie was starting the ninth grade in high school.

Billie made April wear the jumper outfit April had stolen from Strouss Department store that past summer.

"You and Renee got your little fast behinds in trouble with that trifling 'Thomas' girl.

Out there stealing clothes like you ain't got no sense. She's back in reform school where she belongs. You're lucky you and Renee ain't locked up too. Well, I had to pay for that little worthless mess, so you're going to wear it."

April hated that jumper. But she wasn't about to argue with Billie. "What would Joey think of me stealing?" she wondered.

* * *

April and Renee were quiet as they walked to school. April could feel Renee staring at her. They would both turn twelve in a couple of weeks and would be the youngest ones in their class. All summer they had talked excitedly about new clothes, starting junior high school and meeting new boys. Now everything had changed. They kicked the brown and gold leaves listlessly in their path in silence.

"My mom won't let me wear mine." She eyed April's outfit. "You look nice."

April knew it fit her well, she had been excited about wearing it, to show off her newly developing figure. Over the summer, she had slimmed down and developed real breasts and was wearing a real bra instead of a trainer. But all that was like some background story now, none of it mattered. She could not feel any of the old excitement. A gray cloud of sorrow hung over her head and she knew it had extended itself to Renee even while Renee tried to put up a good front.

"Thanks, Reny, but I just don't care. Besides, we were really stupid to be out there trying to shop-lift with Mary Thomas."

"We didn't really do it," said Renee. "Mary got the stuff for us, remember?"

"Yeah, I know. But it was still stupid. We could be sittin' up in reform school right now too."

Renee gave April a sidelong glance.

"Why did he do it, April? Why did he kill Joey? And right in front of little Sandy like that. He must be crazy."

April couldn't bear to talk about it but Renee was her best friend.

"Billie says he was real jealous. That's why Joey couldn't go anywhere. He used to time her when she went to the store and stuff like that. And he didn't want her over at our house."

"Her own family?"

"Yeah, that's why she was gonna leave him."

"He must really be crazy!"

"The last time she brought Sandy over, Sandy's leg was in a cast. Joey told Billie that Sandy fell down the steps. But later Sandy told us that Boleo did it."

"Did what?"

"Made her fall."

"They should give him the electric chair."

"He never liked Sandy anyway. You know she's not really his?"

"Yeah, but still..."

"And Billie says he was a lot older than Joey."

"How old is he?"

"Forty-four."

"Wow. And Joey was twenty…"

"Twenty-four"

"Why did she marry a man that old?"

"Oh girl, I don't know." April felt like crying, she wished desperately that they were talking about someone else like always and she didn't feel this lump in her throat.

"I'm so sorry, April," said Renee. "I just can't believe it. "I feel so bad for your whole family. Momma does too. Remember last year when Kennedy died and how sad we were? Seems like the whole world has changed, don't it Apr?" Renee was trying desperately to make some sense of it all and connect with her friend.

"Hey," she said, "Momma said to see if you wanted to spend a few days at our house.

Come on, please."

"You know I would," April said slowly. "But I really don't think I should leave Losie, she doesn't like to sleep by herself, she'll just worry Billie."

April didn't add that Billie didn't like her spending a lot of time at Renee's because Ms Barnett cursed like nobody's business and even though Billie could out-curse the best of them, she didn't believe in cursing kids, it wasn't right. Billie said she didn't want to have to come over there and break Ms Barnett's neck for cursing April, so it was best that April didn't sleep over. Billie didn't feel that it was a good thing to be running in and out of other people's houses anyway, but she never seemed to mind Renee and her other friends spending time at their place.

* * *

April didn't tell Losie about seeing Joey because she knew it would frighten her, but she longed to tell Billie only she didn't know how because she could see the strain that Billie was under trying to shield her and Losie from the gossip out there. Everyone was talking about the shameful way Boleo had shot Joey in cold blood in front of her little girl. It threatened to get the best of Billie, but she stood her ground as usual.

"You girls don't pay any attention to these ignorant ass folks around here, they don't know what they're talking about. Always keep your chin up, don't let them see you weep."

* * *

That year when Thanksgiving arrived, relatives came from all over. Pittsburgh, New York, Cleveland, even relatives from down South who rarely came. A cousin who had been in Germany for years where her husband was stationed made it her business to come home. She made him come with her. Billie's brother Jack said these were all the people who felt guilty because they hadn't come for Joey's funeral.

On Thanksgiving Day, the women gathered in the kitchen to help prepare the meal while the men retired to the den to watch the game and drink Uncle Jack's famous homemade peach brandy.

The kitchen was alive with smells of sweet potato pie and roast turkey. April sat at the table cutting celery, green peppers and onions in tiny cubes the way

Billie had taught her. From the corner of her eye she caught a glimpse of kelly green and looked up. Perched on the little white utility table next to the refrigerator sat Joey. No drama, nothing, just sitting there smiling. She wore her favorite kelly green dress that flared at the waist.

"Joey... Billie, Billie, Joey is here." April dashed across the floor, over-turning her chair, spilling a few cubes of onions.

Billie intercepted her. "What's wrong with you girl, stop that."

The women in the kitchen froze in silence.

"She's right there," April's voice quivered as she pointed and struggled to release herself from Billie's grasp, but Billie held her firmly.

"It's all right now," Billie crooned. "You're Billie's big girl now." Billie pulled April to her, crushing April's face against her soft breasts.

In that vulnerable position, April whispered her secret to Billie, how she'd seen Joey the other day and how frightened she'd been. She kept her voice low, not wanting the women to hear her and think her a silly child. As she spoke, April's eyes were as wide as a female deer when she peered over her mother's shoulder. Joey remained perched next to the refrigerator but now she was pulsating like before, fading in and out, that disturbing ebb and flow. April couldn't look anymore, she hid her face in Billie's comforting breasts and began to cry.

"Shh! Hush now." Billie's voice was soothing. "She came to me too, baby. Offered me the little bouquet of roses. It's only Sandy, April. She just wants us to take care of Sandy, she don't want Boleo's sorry-ass family to have her. That's what the little bouquet is, it's just Sandy," Billie spoke her words boldly, matter-of-factly. She didn't mind that the women heard her. April gaped about the kitchen for gasp of horror and disbelief. There were none.

"Hush now." Billie stroked April's soft braids as she shook her head from side to side, unable to stop her own tears.

"She just wants us to look after Sandy, that's all. She'll rest now."

The women in the kitchen emerged from their silence and came forth and hugged Billie and April as if they understood. Then they moved about the kitchen busily preparing the meal as if nothing had happened.

FRIENDS

Johanna and I were sitting at the bar at Frieda's quietly sipping daiquiris, thinking our separate thoughts when my cousin, Craig, descended upon us with another of his police buddies.

As usual, he was going to try and fix me up. Every since my divorce two years ago, Craig felt compelled to hook me up with someone. It was always one of the brothers that worked with him at the county police department. I loved Craig dearly, but I hated what he did for a living, the danger, the ugliness he encountered daily, and most of all the resulting jaded attitude of him and his fellow officers. They were downright crude to me and Lord knows, I was no angel. But Craig thought I didn't know what I wanted, so he kept trying.

This particular brother Craig had with him tonight was white and I thought surely he had lost his mind. He'd mentioned him to me a few days before, when he came by my office, but at the time I was preoccupied with some paperwork and wasn't really paying him much attention.

"He's white but he's cool, likes black women, was married to one," he'd said. As if that made everything all right. "Looking for a nice lady, that's why I told him about you. Trust me, babe, you know I want nothing but the best for you." I had to smile, it was true. Craig was only two years older than me and every since I can remember, he's been like the big brother I never had. Our fathers were brothers and Craig had two older brothers but I was an only child. They all looked out for me but Craig and I were the closest.

Usually, I went along with Craig's little cupid games by agreeing to double date with him and one of the guys on the force. But it was always the same – never went anywhere. Most of the time, they were nice enough, eager to please, but nothing ever happened. I knew it was my fault and didn't care. I was wary of any relationship since my divorce.

This brother's name was Scott. Now he motioned Scott from the other end of the bar and made a big deal out of it. Craig always was loud.

"This is my beautiful cousin, man. Didn't I tell ya? Didn't I tell ya?"

Scott smiled, even whites gleaming like he was in a TV commercial.

"Nice to meet ya, Jo... Joanna is it?"

"Johanna," I said.

"Johanna," he said, as though savoring it. "That's an unusual name."

"I was named for my mother, she's from Ghana," I said. "This is my friend, Rachel.

"What's happenin' Rachel? How you doin'?"

"Fine," Rachel said. She gave him a sidelong glance. Rachel wasn't very fond of cops either, black or white. She and Craig had a sort of on-again, off-again relationship because she was afraid to get close to him since he was a cop and he showed a deep distrust for women, but at the same time he seemed to

74

feel something for her and always made her laugh. Both of them indulged in other relationships but always seemed to be in a corner whispering and being intimate. I gave up on trying to figure out what they were into long ago. I just knew that Rachel was as wary as I was, being divorced herself.

After a little small talk among the four of us, Craig grabbed Rachel and headed toward the dance floor. I found Scott easy to talk to. He began talking about his ex-wife and when I asked if they'd had kids, he whipped out his wallet containing two cute, light brown kids, a boy and a girl. His face went soft as he spoke about being separated from them. Then he talked about his ex.

"I went through a lot to marry that girl. My folks had money. Cut me off when I married her. Just about killed my mother. And Dad never relented, wouldn't give me a dime. It hurt, but I didn't look back. Loved her."

"What happened?" I asked, not truly wanting to know, but thinking he was going to go there anyway.

"Couldn't stand livin' in the life. As a cop's wife, I mean. She was afraid all the time. I used to work undercover a lot, busting dealers and things like that you know."

Yeah, I knew. "Wanted me to give it up. Begged me to give it up. Couldn't do it. She was asking me to give up my life. I love what I do. So she finally left me."

Scott was tall and muscular with deep brown eyes that crinkled with crows feet at the edges when he smiled. He'd had something done with his hair, it was thick-blond and kinky, a blond Afro. He sprinkled his dialogue with black expressions. I understood what Craig meant, he acted black. He over-did it though, reminded me of some light-skinned brother trying to prove his blackness.

"May I see you again?" He made his voice casual, but I knew he wanted an answer before Craig and

Rachael returned and they were making their way back to the bar. I made him wait.

Craig ordered another round for everyone and then bent over whispering in Rachel's ear. Scott finally asked if I'd go to lunch with him on Monday. I accepted because I couldn't think fast enough to come up with an excuse.

I admit, as Monday approached, I had to go deep within myself. Why in the world had I agreed to see this man again? I wore no makeup, wore my hair natural, always had to have my big gold hooped earrings and on any given day, my wardrobe leaned heavily toward African/Indian. Brightly colored tunics, head-raps, dashikis and loose-flowing dresses were my thing. Chocolate brown and thick-lipped, I knew I wasn't the type of high-yellow black woman with flowing 'good' hair usually found on the arm of a white brother. In short, I considered myself a black woman in the truest sense, so I wasn't ready for this, but curiosity got the best of me.

A county social worker knows she cannot make definite lunch plans, something always comes up. This time was no exception. When Scott showed up I was tied up with a client and completely unaware of the time. I kept him waiting about thirty-five minutes and we settled on the little coffee shop next door.

Scott's eyes danced in amusement as my co-workers stared at us.

"We seem to be the center of attraction," he said.

A sister at the table next to us just stared, she didn't even flinch when I looked her way. Scott winked at her.

"What's happenin'?" he grinned at her. She rolled her eyes and turned away.

"Scott," I said, "I don't like this kind of attention."

"Doesn't bother me, I'm used to it," he said.

But he wasn't used to me, nor I him. He drummed his fingers on the table nervously. I fumbled in my purse for a cigarette. I hadn't anticipated my reaction sitting across from him in the daylight with no booze to cloud my perception. As I attempted to light my cigarette, he took the lighter from my hand and lit it for me. At the touch of his hand, I trembled. He took both of my hands and held them. His hands were big and warm and hairy. I looked at him, questioning.

He stared back at me, searching my face and my eyes.

"I'll just get some coffee," I said. I tried to pull my hands away. He motioned a waiter with his head, still holding on to my hands.

"Two coffees," he said, "I'll take mine black." He looked at me.

"Cream and sugar," I said. "Is there anything you don't like black?" He laughed a deep rich laugh and we both relaxed.

Before long, Scott and I began meeting at the club regularly. One night he invited me to his apartment for dinner. He'd prepared steaks on the grill, baked potatoes and a salad. I guess he figured he couldn't go wrong with that menu. Afterwards we had brandy and listened to some jazz. Scott's apartment was tastefully furnished with lots of black art. I just shook my head in wonder.

At this point, I must tell you that although I'm adventurous, I don't like to sleep around. And for the life of me, I can't remember a specific point when I decided to sleep with Scott that night. I had quite a bit of brandy, but I also found Scott attractive because he seemed genuinely interested in pleasing me all the time. Despite his macho, super-black attitude, he treated me like a lady in the old fashion way and this was refreshing to me. During our lovemaking I couldn't refrain from thinking that it was no different than being with a black man except that he was extremely hairy, thick blond hair on his chest and long thin slivers on his arms and the back of his hands. But his smell, his touch was just that of a man. He was also a very gentle man.

Later as we lay in Scott's king sized bed, he chuckled softly to himself.

"What's funny?"

I lay there relaxing with my eyes closed as Scott puffed on a cigarette. He leaned closer looking down at me, his elbow propped on a pillow.

"I was just thinking, my Moms would have a fit if she knew she was going to be cleaning up after a black woman tomorrow." He laughed again.

I froze. Did he think this was amusing? What *was* he thinking?

"What do you mean, Scott?" My teeth were clinched.

"Well, she cleans my apartment a couple times a week, thinks I can't take care of myself. Anyway, if she knew she was cleaning up behind a black woman, she would freak. I'm tempted to tell her just to see her reaction." This really broke him up. He dropped his head in his pillow and just cracked up.

"What!" I was livid. "So your lily-white momma is so racist that she'd go off if she knew a black woman slept here. That's what you're really saying, isn't it?"

Scott turned back to me, his laughter quickly replaced with a look of concern. I could see his mind working, trying to decide how best to proceed with this. He realized he'd made a mistake. Actually, I was surprised at the strength of my own reaction but I couldn't stop myself.

"Come on, Jo. That was supposed to be funny. Don't start tripping on me."

"Look," I said. "You think you can crinkle your hair into a 'fro and talk black shit and then it's okay for you to lay here and tell me how much your mother hates black folk. I don't see the humor in that. Tell you the truth, your mother sounds like one of those old white women who used to work my grandmother to death in her kitchen for slave wages and then try to give her leftover scraps from her precious table to take home."

Scott looked incredulous. "Jo… baby, don't be so sensitive." He pulled me close. "You've got to meet her, it's not as bad as you think. She's still somewhat of a racist, but…"

"Somewhat of a racist, what the hell is that?" I pulled away from him.

"Okay, look, maybe I can't make you understand that but hey, guess what… she loves her little black grandkids and deep down inside she knows I love black women. It's something in me, I love the golden brown, the chocolate brown, the creamy beige of women of color, always have. My Mom knows deep down that that's who I am and whatever makes me happy she's willing to accept." He pulled me close again. "You know they say that a white man and a black woman are the two most free people in the world."

"Yeah, and whoever said that shit must have assumed that the white man has no conscious and the black woman has no soul. This is ridiculous, Scott. I'm too black for you, you don't have a clue, walking around as if you're black. You're the worst kind of fraud." I regretted being there, this had been a mistake.

"Oh the lady is so serious," said Scott. "I love your passion, your anger… but we're just two people, you can't change the world." He kissed my cheek. "Let's take a shower." He pulled me off the bed and into the large bathroom. We caught our reflection in the full-length mirror and stood still. My breasts stood high and pointed and so did my huge natural 'fro. Scott's artificial 'fro stood just as high and nappy, but he was so pale, the contrast was amazing. My mouth curled into a grin first. Scott looked at me and started smiling and pulled us both closer to the mirror. Before we knew it we were both laughing hysterically.

"Chocolate and vanilla cake," said Scott. "We're beautiful, we're beautiful."

I pulled Scott back to the bed where we made love and laughed some more.

Finally, I said, "Let's not make this complicated Scott. Let's just be friends."

"Can't we all just get along," he said, teasing me.

"I'm serious," I said.

"I know you are, baby. You're always serious." Scott sighed deeply.

"I guess I'll just have to accept that," he said.

He did. And unto this day that's what we are, we're friends.

MENA THE GROUPIE

Mena stepped briskly from the bus and darted to the escalator. It was only 9:00 a.m. but she wanted to make sure she caught the next train to the Lenox station. She wanted to avoid the crowd of leisure shoppers that was sure to descend upon Macy's before noon. She was glad that she'd taken an entire day off from work last week to shop for her outfit. Now all she needed was accessories.

Mena boarded the Northbound train, claimed the nearest seat and sat back to relax and enjoy the ride. She hoped no one would sit next to her because she wanted to think about the wonderful night ahead.

Brent had phoned two weeks earlier and she couldn't wait to see him. His group was scheduled to do a gig at the Fox theatre for the Christmas weekend and he definitely wanted to see her. They'd been seeing each other on and off for about five years. More precisely, Mena had made it her business to be at every show when Brent and The Faculty performed. For years they played the local clubs in and around

Pennsylvania and Ohio. Mena had been there at the Front Row in Cleveland the night the group opened for some big name. Brent later told her that someone really big was in the audience that night. From that point on The Faculty took off. Before long they were touring the country and Mena began receiving airline tickets in the mail. Brent was married and had two children, but Mena went anyway.

"I'm crazy about you, baby," Brent would say. "You're so fine." Then he would take her shopping for jewelry and sexy dresses. "You like spending my money, don't you, baby?"

"You know you like to see me look good, you my big Teddy bear, my Big Daddy," Mena would say. She'd smile sweetly and kiss him on the eyelids the way he liked. They'd end up back at the hotel where the group was partying. By this time there'd be other selected females who'd attended the show. Beautiful women. Getting high, making love. The Faculty had anything the women wanted to feel good. Soon Mena would urge Brent to take her elsewhere. She felt above these women, she and Brent had something going. She'd whisper in his ear and soon they'd leave. He'd wine and dine her before taking her to another lavish hotel to make love.

A year ago he'd asked her to marry him. She'd laughed lightly.

"You're still married, remember? You're trying to mess with my head, right?"

"Listen to me." He pulled her to him, held her face. "I'm divorcing her. Trust me, baby. Say you'll marry me. I can give you anything you want. I love you," he pleaded. Mena withdrew from him and stepped back with her hands on her hips.

"Come on, Big Daddy, I'm not ready for marriage. Anyway, I'm moving to Atlanta soon. I want to go into business for myself, open up a little boutique, you know? But we can still see each other like always."

"I can help you, Mena, you know that," said Brent. He watched her as she moved to the sleek sofa, stretched out and lit a joint, her languid, indifferent eyes resting on something unknown. Brent had never thought her cold until that moment.

After that, there had been no more tickets in the mail. She hadn't heard anything from Brent, until now. Had he divorced and did he still want her? She didn't know what to expect.

At Macy's she'd picked up a red slinky number, Brent's favorite color. Red spiked heels, red panties and a push-up bra. Brent would want to undress her.

* * *

That evening, Brent sent someone for her. He'd phoned early that morning. She'd spent the early evening pampering herself. Hair, nails and feet. When the limousine arrived, Mena stunned the driver with her blood-red attire. She was radiant. At the theatre, she was led to special seating up front with significant others of the group. They were already in concert when she arrived. Mena had hoped to have a moment with Brent before the show, but traffic had been nightmarish.

The crowd was festive and glitzy with holiday cheer. When The Faculty ended its fine version of 'Silent Night', Brent began talking into the microphone.

"I'd like to send this out to a very special lady, someone whom I'll always care for." With that he began to belt out 'A Song for Donny,' a beautiful tribute to Donny Hathaway originally recorded by The Whispers. Brent knew it was Mena's favorite. The sisters in the crowd went wild; Brent took them to church with his moving rendition. Mena had tears in her eyes. She stood with her hands in the air, enraptured.

Brent's entourage swept Mena up at the end of the show. Apparently, the 'Who's Who' of black Atlanta was throwing a Christmas party at the Peachtree Westin Hotel and they insisted that The Faculty attend.

Before she knew it, Mena was seated in another limousine with Brent at her side. He held a glass of champagne for her. She shook her head, she didn't need it. With one gulp he emptied the glass. He watched her as they drove through downtown Atlanta, his eyes twinkling like the lights on the skyline.

"I've missed you Brent."

Brent raised a brow, then smiled.

"I'll bet you have," he said.

Mena wanted to hear him say he'd missed her, but he took her in his arms instead. He kissed her harshly, bruising her mouth. Then gently he kissed her neck, her forehead, her hair, her lids. She lifted her hand to guide his mouth and he grabbed it and kissed it too.

* * *

In the past year, Mena had turned thirty, but she could still pass for twenty to the untrained eyed. Short and trim, Mena almost looked boyish when her hair was cropped off. But it grew back fast and was now at its' normal shoulder length. She wore it straight, jet black with blond streaks in the front. Her breasts were small and her hips were not impressive but she had nice legs and knew how to accentuate them. Always, she wore short skirts and dresses with spike heels. And perfume, her hair always had a hint of perfume.

Mena had grown up with three older brothers and when she was small, they used her for a punching bag. But as she blossomed into a teenager, they became protective of her. Her father showered her with clothes and gifts just as he did her mother. He was a foreman in the steel mill and though they weren't rich by any stretch of the imagination, he always brought all his money home.

Mena's momma ruled by example. She showed Mena how to handle men. She was petite and demure also, and no one expected her of being intelligent. This worked in her favor and she hid it well. It didn't take Mena long to pick up on her momma's cues.

As a young woman, the men in Mena's life treated her like a fragile doll—initially anyway. She knew how to make them spend money on her and they would oblige as long as she was good to them. Mena rarely worked. Sometimes she'd take a secretarial job from a temp agency when she had a particular goal in mind; a trip to Atlanta for example. When she had the money she needed, she'd quit. Her regular living expenses were paid for by the men in her life. Sometimes she lived with them, but mostly she kept her own place. Mena saw nothing wrong with this, to her it was just a way of life. A way to survive until the right man came along.

"Mena, don't you want to have children?" her best friend, Jeanette once asked. "Men are always after you, what are you looking for?"

"Honey, I'm not about to ruin my body having nobody's baby any time soon, okay. A baby is the last thing on my mind. As for what I'm looking for, I'll let you know when I find it." One thing about Mena, she didn't like folks getting into her business, she'd tell you where to get off in a heartbeat. She'd never told Jeanette that she'd already had two abortions. Both mistakes. She'd been careless. She wasn't about to be tied down. The thing was, she liked younger men. She liked to smell their baby breath as it blew on her cheek when they slept after making love. She liked teaching them how to make love to her. And she enjoyed seeing the raw passion that they hadn't yet learned to conceal.

The men who gave her money, the older men, were always possessive, always drunk and they hurt her with their big callous hands and with their coarse stubbled chin buried in her breasts. She could never marry one of them. She would get whatever she could from them and when their possessiveness got out of control, she would leave. Quietly, softly, she would make her move in the middle of the night. She never looked back.

Once, she'd tried to make Jeanette understand how she felt.

"Girl, you're crazy, you just want control, that's all. I love the roughness of a man. As long as he's not trying to hurt me. That's part of a man's nature." She had looked at Mena as if Mena had grown horns. Mena knew then that she didn't understand.

Brent fit into that 'older man' category, but he had been gentle during their lovemaking. Mena liked that about him. She'd done some deep thinking in this past year. She'd taken a hiatus from her usual lifestyle. Took a full-time job. Paid her own rent. She'd looked from left to right at her friends and all the people she knew. Many had lived the life she lived but had long given it up. Others were married with children or had careers or both. Mena felt she had nothing, except her looks. But that was no longer enough. She wanted a husband, a child. Sometimes she dreamed that she and Brent were married and living the life of the rich, traveling around the world with The Faculty. In an alternate dream, she stayed behind while he toured and ran her own boutique while they planned a family.

* * *

"You still want me, Brent?' Mena asks.

"Of course," says Brent. He looks uncomfortable.

"I mean… do you still want to marry me?" They were back at the hotel.

"I've met someone, Mena. We're going to get married. I wanted to let you know that."

"When were you going to tell me, after you fucked my brains out tonight." Mena couldn't help it, all the trouble she'd gone through to get herself together for this man, all the money she'd spent on her clothes to please him, shit, who did he think he was.

"You seem to be doing alright for yourself, girl. Made your move to Atlanta, still looking good. He remembered how she'd blown him off when he saw her last, her coldness.

"I loved you girl, would have done anything for you. Put you on a pedestal, thought you were different from those other groupies, whores or whatever you want to call them. But naw, you played me for a chump, just wanted my money. Mena the groupie, know what I'm saying? Shoulda been smarter than that. But I still care about you, wanted to see you again, how you were doing..."

"And tell me you're getting married. Thanks a lot, Brent." Mena gained her composure somewhat. "I've changed Brent. I know what I want now."

"Sure baby, let's make love, forget all that serious stuff." He pulled her close.

"Take me home, Brent. I need to go home." She turned away to hide the glassiness in her eyes.

"We just got here, girl. Come on, don't tell me you can't have fun with me anymore. I thought we still had that. Life is too short, don't take it so serious."

She stared at him with a sense of detachment. Her mind was racing. So this is how it was. Timing was everything. Opportunity doesn't knock often and Mena knew she'd blown it. Something inside her withered, she'd put such hope in this reunion. Something was wrong with this picture. He was the one who should be groveling, not her.

"Take me home," Mena says.

"Okay, okay!" Brent wasn't the least bit angry, he seemed almost relieved.

* * *

They were parked in front of Mena's apartment.

"Nice seeing you again, baby. Hope things work out for you and I wish you the best."

"Nice seeing you too, Brent." Mena was livid and it was all she could do to contain herself, his self-assurance and goodwill only added to her humiliation.

"If you ever need anything—don't hesitate to call me, okay?"

"Yeah, okay, Brent." Mena slams his car door without looking back as she makes her way to her door. Maybe he thought this shit was over, but he had another think coming. She would get him back – somehow. He wasn't married *yet*. She *should* take his ass on the Jerry Springer show. Yeah! Now *that* was an idea. Mena's mind went into overdrive planning her next move.

MERRY CHRISTMAS TO YOU, TOO

April's Sister

Dec. 23, 1990

Terry stands in the middle of the floor in Macy's waiting for Elliot. He'd promised to meet her.

"Get whatever you want," he'd said.

She checks her watch, wondering what's keeping him as she browses through the coats on the rack.

"May I help you?" a clerk asks.

"Oh no, I'm just looking right now," says Terry. She turns as Elliot taps her on the shoulder.

"Hey babe, how you doing? That one looks good on you. Let's pay for it and get the hell out of here. I've got some last minute running around to do."

Terry checks her reflection in the mirror. She definitely does not like the coat.

"Burgundy just isn't my color. Let me look some more," she says.

Something catches Elliot's attention across the room.

"Get what you want babe, I've got to go." He whips out his wallet and shoves two bills into her hand.

"What's up Elliot?"

He stalks off without answering. Terry follows him with her eyes. He stops near the exit, next to a heavy-set woman admiring a dress. The woman turns to acknowledge him and though Terry's never seen her, she knows it's his wife. It's in Elliot's eyes. Terry stands paralyzed, smells from the perfume counter suddenly stifling. She stuffs the bills in her purse and hurries toward the exit.

* * *

Weaving through the heavy holiday traffic Terry wonders when exactly had Elliot stolen her heart. She'd been twenty when they met three years before. Sure of herself and what she wanted. Friends had warned her that married men were taboo, she'd get hurt. She'd laughed at them. They were the ones who always saw the glass as

105

being half empty. She was on a mission. She wasn't interested in love, she'd been burned once, had a son with no father as a result. It had been a mistake. After that she just wanted to make a better life for her son and maybe a little bit of excitement. Elliot could give her that. She was working full-time and taking college courses at night. Elliot bought her things, made her laugh and sometimes even paid her bills. She had nicer things than most of her friends. But now she has the feeling that something is about to be snatched from her, that old sense of deprivation, of being abandoned. Seeing his wife had brought it home to her – he really was married and her need for him is painful. She is frightened for the first time.

Terry turns the key in her apartment door. From below, her friend Ruth yells up the stairs. "What'cha doing tonight? Got plans?"

Terry sighs and answers as cheerfully as she can, "No, I'm about to shower and get a quick bite, that's all."

"Johnny's asleep already, may as well let him stay tonight," says Ruth. She's at the bottom of the stairwell.

"No Elliot tonight?" Ruth can't stand Elliot but she sees something in Terry's face and lets it go.

"How about a couple of cocktails. My turkey's already in the oven, maybe we can capture that elusive Christmas spirit."

Terry seriously doubts Ruth's last statement, but she agrees reluctantly. She liked Ruth a lot and felt Ruth was really sweet to keep Johnny for her and charge her so little, less than she did for the other four children she kept. They'd become close, but an inspiration Ruth was not. Ruth was always depressed by her own admission and regularly went for counseling. As a result, she had this idea that if you talked it out, cried it out, leaving out no sordid little detail, it was good for your psyche. But her spirits would miraculously soar as soon as you revealed your troubles. She'd suddenly sparkle like gold and her 'good advice' would spring forth like that of an inspirational speaker.

Terry decides on a simple salad as she removes her small turkey from the freezer to thaw.

Ruth lets herself in just as Terry finishes the dishes. Terry mixes daiquiris as Ruth rattles on about this brother she is seeing. She's glad Ruth's in the mood to talk, that way she doesn't have to.

The phone rings. "I'm on my way over," Elliot says.

"No, Elliot, I don't want to see you tonight." Terry hangs up.

"What's the deal with you and Elliot?" Ruth's eyes are wide.

Reluctantly, Terry explains what happened.

"Did she see you?" Ruth asks.

"No, I don't think so, she wouldn't know me anyway."

There's a soft knock on the door. Terry knows it's Elliot, he never rings the bell. Ruth watches her as she goes to the door. Elliot bounces in and pulls her into his arms. She pushes him away and he strides across the room ignoring Ruth, picks up a shot glass, pours himself some rum and drinks it straight.

"Merry Christmas to you, too," Ruth says. "I'll just disappear." She rolls her eyes at Terry on her way out the door.

Aretha's crooning 'Darling You Send Me' on the CD player, an old Sam Cooke tune. Terry loves old music.

Elliot kneels in front of her as she reclines on the white leather loveseat.

"I'm sorry about what happened today, baby. It was just one of those things. I don't understand it, my wife never shops at Macy's." He tilts her chin, forcing her to look at him.

"Forgive me?"

Terry doesn't answer.

Terry's spacious living area is covered with forest green carpet; there are various lush large plants, mirrors, crystal and chimes in strategic places. Terry believes in Fung Shui, an ancient Buddhist practice of harnessing a flow of balance in one's surroundings to create harmony. The Christmas tree in front of the patio window has miniature flashing lights and small crystals dangling from it. Snow sprinkles lightly outside the patio window. Outside, the night is navy blue.

"I have something to tell you," says Elliot.

Terry looks at him, her mouth set.

"I'm not well, Terry."

Terry's expression does not change.

"I may not have long." He lowers his head.

"What are you talking about?"

"I'm sick baby, I've known it for a while. Now the doctor tells me I don't have long. I'm only telling you this because I need you, I don't want to lose you, Terry."

They sit quietly as if meditating. The wind chimes above the patio tinkle. The smell of Ruth's turkey makes Terry's nose twitch. She wishes she was still listening to Ruth, she didn't want to hear this. She doesn't know what to feel, what to say.

"Elliot, I…"

"Shh. Don't say anything right now."

Terry lowers herself on the floor with him and he enfolds her in his arms.

* * *

She wakes with a start, the feeling that someone has just spoken or made a noise. She looks around, naturally Elliot's gone. He has this ritual which dictated that he never stay the entire night, he always left before dawn.

Terry showers and makes coffee with thoughts of Elliot's lovemaking on her mind, she closes her eyes and feels his touch. But strangely, she feels no sadness. Certain memories form in her mind. She fumbles through the kitchen cupboard, looks over her Christmas dinner menu and decides to pick up a few things. Johnny's still asleep. She decides to walk, she needs fresh air.

Outside, everything appears clean and new with fresh white snow resting upon it. Children are running and throwing snowballs at each other. Decorations adorn every window, Terry feels alive and fresh as the snow. She laughs. People stare at her and she doesn't care. Elliot. He had lied again. She knew it as sure as she knew her own name. Just as he had lied so many other times. She remembers the time he told her that there was a death in his family in Pennsylvania. Naturally, she gave her condolences and he'd told her he'd be gone for a week. At the time she'd thought, at least she had plans. She and Ruth were going to a Stevie Wonder concert.

"Enjoy it baby, I'll see you next week," he'd said.

And she did, but as it turned out, not as much as Ruth and another girlfriend. In retrospect, it was actually humorous to Terry too. She'd torn one of her contacts on the day of the concert but was determined to go and have a good time anyway. Elliot, himself, was there with another woman (not his wife) and everyone saw him but Terry. With only one contact, she'd seen a blur of a man who stood above the crowd because of his height and for a brief moment she thought it was Elliot. No one said anything until much later and of course, Terry had felt like a fool. Then there had been the time when this woman knocked on her door looking for him – yet another woman – and he'd hidden in the closet.

Terry puts the last touches on her turkey and closes the oven. Johnny's bouncing around the tree with excitement over his new toys. Terry goes to the window as a car door slams. Elliot is walking toward the apartment with that confident air of his. She opens the door.

"Merry Christmas," he says. There's a large package in his hands. "Something extra for you, babe."

Terry flashes him her most radiant smile. "It's over, Elliot. Take your package and get out." She shoves him gently.

His face flashes surprise, then suspicion, before he gets himself together.

"You can't quit me."

"What the hell do you mean, I can't quit you. Get out!"

"Women don't let me go, I let them go." There is amusement in his eyes.

"Just go Elliot," Terry says wearily. "I'm tired of your games." She shoves him again.

"You can't do this baby, it's Christmas, you'll be sorry as soon as I leave." This time Terry shoves him out the door.

"Go home to your wife, she deserves you." She slams the door in his face.

Elliot bangs on the door.

"Don't be so childish, Terry. Let's talk about this."

Terry doesn't answer and after a few minutes she hears him descend the stairs.

"Mommy, what's wrong?" By this time, little Johnny's leaning against the kitchen entrance, wide eyed.

"Nothing baby." She swoops him up in her arms, kisses him, and moves toward the window. Elliot's standing at his car looking up at her. She doesn't move. He starts back toward the apartment, changes his mind, turns back, jumps into his car and drives away. Terry remains at the window. Silently, she forms his name with her lips.

About the Author

Social Worker living in Atlanta Ga. Poems published in 'Rymes of Greatness' anthology published by 'Famous Poets Society' and 'Hotlanta News Magazine'.